The Animal Kingdom

ANIMAL ADAPTATIONS

Malcolm Penny

Illustrated by Vanda Baginska

The Bookwright Press
New York · 1989

The Animal Kingdom

Animal Adaptations
Animal Camouflage
Animal Defenses
Animal Evolution
Animal Homes
Animal Migration
Animal Movement

Animal Partnerships
Animal Reproduction
Animal Signals
Animals and their Young
Endangered Animals
The Food Chain
Hunting and Stalking

First published in the
United States in 1989 by
The Bookwright Press
387 Park Avenue South
New York, NY 10016

First published in 1988 by
Wayland (Publishers) Ltd
61 Western Road, Hove
East Sussex BN3 1JD, England

Library of Congress Cataloging-in-Publication Data

Penny, Malcolm
   Animal adaptations / Malcolm Penny.
     p. cm. — (The animal kingdom)
   Bibliography: p.
   Includes index.
   Summary: Describes how animals have adapted
themselves in appearance and behavior to survive a
variety of conditions and climates.
   ISBN 0–531–18222–3
1. Adaptation (Biology)—Juvenile literature. [1.
Adaptation (Biology) 2. Animals—Habits and behavior.]
I. Title.
II. Series: Penny, Malcolm. Animal kingdom.
QP82.P37 1989
599.05–dc 19

                        88–6897
                            CIP
                            AC

Typeset by DP Press, Sevenoaks, Kent, England
Printed by Casterman SA, Belgium

All the words printed in **bold** are
explained in the glossary on page 30.

Contents

What is an adaptation?

An adaptation is something about an animal that makes it possible for it to live in a particular place and in a particular way. It may be a physical adaptation, like the size or shape of the animal's body, or the way in which its body works. Or it may be the way the animal behaves. Each adaptation has been produced by **evolution**.

As the **environment** changes, animals that cannot adapt die out, and only the adapted ones survive to produce babies. Because babies are usually more or less like their parents, the whole **species** soon contains only animals that are adapted to the new environment.

An animal's environment consists of many different things. The climate is important: whether it is hot, cold, dry, or wet will have an effect on all the creatures that live in a particular place.

The beak-like mouth of the parrot fish is an example of a physical adaptation. The fish uses the hard plates of its mouth to gnaw off pieces of coral from the seabed of tropical oceans.

The woodpecker finch of the Galapagos Islands has adapted its behavior in order to find food. Although it does not have a long beak or tongue, like a woodpecker, it can reach insects in tree holes by levering them out with a twig.

Another important part of an animal's environment is what kinds of food plants grow in it. The other animals that live there also have an effect. If there are **predators** around, the **prey** animals will have to learn to defend themselves or run fast to escape.

The greatest example of adaptation took place hundreds of millions of years ago when animals first came out of the sea and began to live on land. They had to be able to breathe oxygen in the air instead of obtaining it from the water. To do this their **gills** gradually changed into lungs. A lung is like a gill tucked into the animal's body. It provides a wet surface where oxygen can be dissolved and picked up by the bloodstream. It has to be inside the body — if it were outside in the air, it would soon dry up and stop working.

The new land animals also had to be able to move around without being supported by water, so new limbs and muscles **evolved**. In this book we shall look at some of the special adaptations that suit animals for the different ways in which they live.

Adaptations to cold climates

The main danger for animals that live in cold places is losing heat into the air. A pea cools down more quickly than a potato because it has more surface area for every gram of its weight. A small animal has more surface area compared with its weight than a large animal, so it loses heat much more quickly. Therefore, in cold climates large animals survive better than small ones.

Being big is not enough. Even very large animals must have some other adaptations to keep warm. Polar bears have thick coats, which keep them warm by trapping a layer of still air next to their skin. Husky dogs and mountain goats also have thick fur or wool for the same reason.

Sea otters have such thick coats that although they are in the cold sea most of the time, their skin never gets wet. Walruses, seals and whales protect themselves from the cold by having a thick layer of fat called blubber, which acts as **insulation**.

With their thick, waterproof fur, sea otters manage to keep warm in the cold seas around Alaska, where they live. Their normal diet consists of sea urchins and large shellfish, but sea otters enjoy eating fish when they can catch them.

Polar bears and arctic foxes have another adaptation to living in the Arctic: they have hair on the soles of their feet, not only to keep them warm but also to prevent them from skidding on the ice.

In the northern parts of Japan, where it can be very cold in the winter, there are hot springs from volcanoes which produce warm water all year round. A species of monkey called the Japanese macaque lives beside the springs, so that it can keep warm in winter by having hot baths.

Reindeer and many birds escape severe winter weather when they **migrate** to warmer countries. Another way of escaping the winter is by hibernating, which means going to sleep in a safe, sheltered place until the spring comes. All kinds of animals hibernate, from large grizzly bears and brown bears in Canada and the United States, to the tiny European dormouse and the pika.

A group of Japanese macaques, or snow monkeys, enjoy a warm bath in a volcanic pool. Many thousands of years ago the first monkey must have tried bathing in such heated pools, while the ground was covered with snow.

Mountain life

Mountain animals must be adapted to their cold and dangerous environment both physically and in their behavior. We have already seen how animals keep warm in cold places, but in the mountains there are other dangers.

The first danger is falling. Animals that live in high rocky or icy places need feet that can firmly grip the ground. In the European Alps the chamois and the ibex have flexible hoofs, which spread apart as the animal walks, giving it a very good grip even on smooth rock. The klipspringer in southern Africa, and the mountain goat in the American Rocky Mountains have very similar hoofs.

When mountain goats hear an **avalanche** coming, they do not run for their lives. Instead, they press themselves close to the cliff. Unless they are very unlucky, the falling snow and rock will pass safely over their heads.

Mountain goats have feet that can grip rocky surfaces. Their kids are less sure-footed, however, so the mother goat stands below her kid on steep slopes in case it slips.

During the winter, mountain goats move farther down the mountainside, where it is warmer and there is less danger of avalanches.

High up in the mountains, there is less oxygen to breathe than at lower levels. This calls for another adaptation, this time to the animal's blood. Animals that live at high **altitude** need to have more red blood cells than those that live lower down. This is because it is the red blood cells that carry oxygen from the lungs around an animal's body to supply its brain and muscles.

Living in the mountains has its advantages as well as its hardships. There is usually less **competition** for food because not many animals can live up there, and there are usually fewer predators. However, there are always a few eagles around, looking for prey. Small mountain animals, such as marmots and pikas, hide from them under piles of rocks at the foot of the cliffs. In the winter they hibernate in the same place with a store of grass, which they use as bedding and food.

Bears living in the mountainous regions of the northern United States and Canada hibernate during the winter. As they sleep in a hidden, sheltered den, they use up very little energy and so survive the very cold weather.

9

Adaptations to hot climates

The jackrabbit of the Arizona desert loses heat through its enormous ears, which are the largest of any American rabbit.

Opposite *A dancing lizard of the Namib desert cools two of its feet in the air. The plants in the background are called welwitschia. They are so well adapted to the desert climate that they may live for a thousand years.*

Desert animals have several adaptations to prevent them from becoming too hot. They must be quite small, to find enough shade and food. Many are **nocturnal** and avoid going out during the day.

There are some animals that can survive for a time in the hot sun. The dancing lizard, which lives in the Namib desert of southern Africa, has to search for food by day because its eyes are not adapted to see in the dark. To avoid burning itself on the sand, it stands with only two feet on the ground, holding the other two in the air. It changes feet from time to time, so the ones it was using can cool off. When the sun becomes too hot, the lizard burrows under the sand to rest in the shade.

Another common adaptation that helps an animal to lose heat is to have large ears with a good blood supply. The fennec fox, which lives in East Africa, and the long-eared hedgehog from the desert of Kuwait, are good examples. In the United States rabbits and hares have longer ears the farther south they live. The jackrabbit of Arizona has the longest ears of all.

The animals best known for losing heat through their ears are the elephants of India and Africa. Their ears have a very good blood supply, and they flap them so that the air cools their blood. Elephants, hippopotamuses and rhinoceroses would seem to be too large to live in a hot country. However, unlike animals that live in deserts, they can cool down by wallowing in muddy pools.

Many animals keep cool by sweating, but for those that do not have many **sweat glands** in their skin, such as cats and dogs, panting is the next best method. In a later chapter we shall see how animals have become adapted to a shortage of water.

10

Solutions to a salty problem

It is very important for all animals to keep their blood at the right **concentration**, neither too salty nor too **dilute**. If an animal controls its body temperature by sweating, it has to replace not only the water that is lost but also the salts that sweat contains. If it does not do so, parts of its body will stop working properly, particularly nerves and muscles, and the animal might suffer from **cramps**.

Many animals use natural salt licks, finding places where they can lick salt from the ground. In national parks in Africa, Canada and the United States, artificial salt licks are often put in a place where people can watch the animals (mostly deer and antelope) when they come to take salt.

For some animals, the opposite is true: their environment contains too much salt, so they must lose some of it. Seabirds have a gland at the base of the bill that removes salt from their blood after they have been feeding or drinking.

An African elephant taking minerals from the earth at a salt lick. It does this to replace the salts it loses from its body.

11705

Mudskippers and fiddler crabs are well suited to tidal changes of the tropical swamps where they live. Mudskippers are able to live in and out of the salt water, whereas fiddler crabs retreat into a waterproof burrow when the tide comes in.

Most fish live either where there is too much salt, in the ocean, or where there is too little, in fresh water. They are adapted to live where they do by having kidneys that remove some of the salt or some of the water, to keep their blood at the right concentration. However, there are some fish, such as eels, trout and salmon, which can move from salt water into fresh and back again. Their kidneys work differently as the fish moves from one place to another.

The hardest place for a water animal to live is in an estuary, where a river flows into the sea. When the tide comes in, the water is salty, and when it goes out, the river brings fresh water to cover the animals.

Ghost crabs, fiddler crabs and a kind of fish called mudskippers all live successfully in saltwater swamps of the tropical regions. One species of monkey in Southeast Asia called the long-tailed macaque is also quite at home in such areas, where it wades into the water to hunt for crabs.

Surviving in dry places

Some animals never drink water at all. Many birds and some lizards manage to obtain all the water they need from **digesting** their food. The Australian koala is famous for not drinking, but getting its water from the eucalyptus leaves it eats.

Camels are well known for storing water in their stomachs for days. Some other desert animals have most unexpected ways of finding or collecting water. In the hot sands of the Namib desert, where the dancing lizard lives, there is a large black beetle that stands on its head every morning. The sea mist that sweeps in every day forms water droplets on the beetle's back, and these trickle down grooves toward its head, so that it can drink.

Even finer grooves run along the back of the thorny moloch lizard, which lives in the deserts of central Australia. Any dew that falls on it, or the slightest shower of rain, is drawn along the grooves to its mouth.

Right *Two silver-backed jackals of Namibia have found a wild melon plant. The fruit is a welcome source of water in this hot, dry area of Africa.*

Below *The Australian koala obtains the water it needs by digesting eucalyptus leaves, which are poisonous to many other animals and people.*

The sand grouse, which lives in dry parts of East and Central Africa, can carry water to its chicks by air. The male parent bird sits in a pool until its breast feathers are soaked, and then flies back to its chicks. They suck the water from the feathers, until they are old enough to fly to fetch their own. Jackals that live in the same area find water by digging up wild melons to eat.

The spadefoot toad lives in the deserts of Arizona, but it spends most of the year asleep under ground. It has a specially adapted skin, which can soak up any water that is in the soil.

One species of mosquito, which lives in African deserts, has the most extraordinary adaptation of all. Its **larvae** can become completely dry and remain so for more than twenty years. They come back to life as soon as water touches them, when they continue their development into adults.

A darkling beetle of the Namib desert drinks the water that has collected on its back from the morning mist.

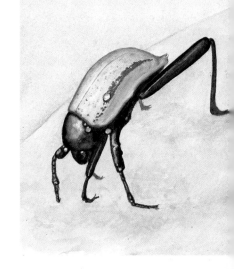

15

Adaptations for flying

The only two groups of animals that can truly fly are birds and bats. They have wings, which they flap to drive themselves through the air. To do this, they need very large muscles in their chests. These heavy muscles hang below the wings, making the animals more stable in the air.

The shape of a wing is very important. It must be fairly flat to provide resistance to the air. The upper surface of a bird's wing bulges slightly upward, while the lower surface is hollow, exactly like the wings of an airplane. This shape provides lift as the wing moves through the air, so that the bird can glide. Bats are less skilled at gliding than birds because their wings are a different shape. Some birds, such as the albatrosses of New Zealand and the vultures of Africa, can glide for several miles without moving their wings at all.

Below left *The diagram shows how air flows over a bird's wing. Air curving over the top of the wing moves faster than air flowing straight under the wing. This means it is at a lower pressure. The higher pressure of the air under the wing produces lift, which keeps the bird in the air.*

Below right *This illustration of the European goldfinch shows the different types of feathers on a bird's wing.*

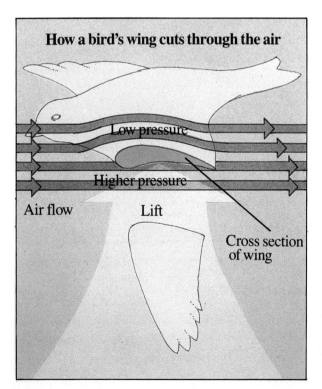

How a bird's wing cuts through the air

Low pressure

Higher pressure

Air flow   Lift

Cross section of wing

The structure of a wing

Contour feathers

Secondary feathers

Primary feathers

Besides their flight feathers (the long, strong ones on their wings and tail) birds are covered with a layer of contour feathers to make their bodies **streamlined**. They also have hollow bones, for lightness, and they have very good eyesight.

While not able to fly like birds and bats, a number of animals can glide for short distances. Many of them live in forests, where it is useful to glide from tree to tree. The gliding frog of Indonesia has very large webs on its feet, which it spreads out when it leaps off a branch. The webs provide resistance to the air, acting like a parachute and slowing the frog down as it falls toward the forest floor. Flying squirrels of Southeast Asia and the Americas, the gliding lemurs of Southeast Asia and even one species of lizard all glide successfully, using flaps of skin that stretch between their front and hind limbs.

A few fish of tropical oceans can fly for short periods to escape an enemy. To do this, they swim fast along the surface of the water, beating it with their tails. Then they spread their huge fins, which enable them to glide through the air.

Flying squirrels are one of the few mammals that can glide, looking rather like a kite. This flying squirrel is found in broadleaved forests of the eastern United States.

Life in the water

Living in water is very different from living in air. Water supports an animal more than air. This means that **mammals** that have returned to the water after living on land, such as the great whales and the manatees, can grow to an enormous size, much bigger than they could on land. If a whale or a manatee becomes stranded on a beach, it will soon die because its muscles are not strong enough to enable it to move or even breathe.

Moving in water is more difficult than moving through the air because the water offers more resistance. Most animals that have become adapted to moving in water are streamlined, shaped rather like fish, so that they can move more easily. Dolphins, otters, platypuses, seals and swimming birds, such as penguins and puffins, are all perfectly suited to the water.

The Australian duck-billed platypus spends most of its time in the water. Its flattened bill, streamlined body and paddle-like tail all give the platypus its streamlined shape, helping it to cut through the water.

Animals that millions of years ago returned to the water from the land have to come to the surface regularly to breathe air. Some of them can hold their breath for a very long time, and dive to great depths. Sperm whales can remain under water for nearly two hours, and dive to over 3,000m (9,800ft) to find their food. The Weddell seal of the Antarctic goes on fishing trips that can last over an hour and take it more than 300m (980ft) below the surface.

Another important adaptation for warm-blooded animals that live in water is to have some way of saving heat. The blubber of whales and seals acts as insulation against the cold oceans where they live, while penguins and seabirds have thick waterproof feathers, which keep a layer of air close to their skin.

The animals mentioned so far are all perfectly adapted to life *in* the water, but there is one creature that can move *on* the water. The basilisk lizard of Central America actually runs across the water surface to escape an enemy. The lizard runs on its hind legs, using its long toes to spread its weight on the water, rather like water skis.

A South American basilisk, or Jesus Cristo, lizard runs across water to escape an enemy. Notice its long toes and tail, which help the lizard to balance on the water.

19

Ruby-throated hummingbird
uses long beak to reach nectar

Feeding adaptations

Dromedary camel has strong teeth
for grinding up vegetation

Animals that eat plants must have a way of collecting them and breaking them up, so they can digest them. Mammal **herbivores** have lips or front teeth to gather their food, and grinding teeth to break it up. Birds that eat plants may have strong beaks to crack nuts and seeds.

Carnivorous animals need sharp beaks or teeth for cutting and tearing meat. Animals that eat fish need to get a firm grip on their slippery prey, so they tend to have specialized teeth or claws, or a saw-like edge to their beaks, like that of a fish-eating duck or a gannet.

Animals that eat nectar must be able to reach this sweet substance at the base of a flower. Bees, butterflies, some moths and the Australian honey possum have long tongues for this purpose, while American hummingbirds and African sunbirds use their long, thin beaks.

Animals are adpated for feeding in many different ways.

Giant anteater uses long
tongue for feeding on termites

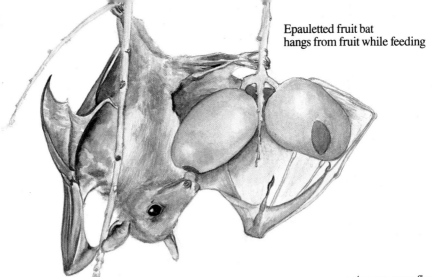

Epauletted fruit bat
hangs from fruit while feeding

Anteaters all over the world have long, thin tongues, which they use to extract termites from their mounds. The Australian echidna, the South American anteaters and the African aardvark all feed in the same way. Woodpeckers have very long tongues for extracting insects from cracks in trees.

The aye-aye, a very rare lemur, which lives in Madagascar, has a long, thin finger on each hand. It uses its finger to extract grubs from under the bark of trees. It also feeds on coconuts, dipping its finger in and licking off the milk. The striped possum of the Australian **rain forest** also has a long, thin finger, which it uses to pick out insects from holes in trees.

Animals that do not have a suitable physical adaptation may have evolved special behavior for collecting certain foods. The woodpecker finch in the Galapagos Islands, off South America, uses a twig held in its beak to dig out grubs in dead wood, making up for the fact that it does not have a long beak or tongue like a woodpecker.

Aye-aye uses fingers
to eat fruit

Fox has sharp teeth
for eating flesh

21

Living in the dark

Some animals move around only at night and sleep in the day. These nocturnal animals need eyes that are specially adapted for seeing in the dark. Lorises, lemurs and bushbabies have enormous round eyes, so they can see perfectly as they move in dark tropical forests at night. Their eyes are this shape and size because they can receive more light.

There are other animals that are adapted to live under the ground or in caves. Moles spend almost all of their lives under ground. They are often thought to be blind, but in fact most of them have tiny eyes, which can at least tell the difference between light and darkness.

True cave animals have no eyes, finding their way about by using other senses, such as smell, hearing and touch. It might seem strange that an animal could grow up without eyes, but it is explained by the continuous process we call evolution.

The European mole has tiny eyes. Good eyesight is not necessary for this underground-dweller, whereas well-developed front paws are essential for digging the mole's burrows.

This cave-dwelling fish has no need for eyes because it lives in total darkness.

Growing eyes while an animal is developing uses up energy, and if the eyes are unnecessary, that energy is wasted. Cave animals have evolved not to grow eyes at all. For the same reason, many of them are white or colorless.

Bats are almost blind, but they avoid bumping into things, and find their prey, by listening for the echoes of sounds that they make themselves. This technique is called sonar after the echo-sounders used by submarines. One bird that uses sonar is the cave swiftlet, which lives all over Southeast Asia. It is the bird whose nests are used in soup.

Swiftlets nest in pitch-dark caves, but far from being blind, they have enormous eyes, which they use for hunting insects when they are flying around outside in the daylight. When they fly into a cave, they change their voices to produce a buzzing sound. They use this as sonar, to help them move around in the total darkness of the caves.

Life in the trees

The animals illustrated here are found in the South American rain forest. Each one is specially adapted to life in the trees.

Animals that live in trees must be good climbers, and they must be well adapted to gripping leaves and branches. The most famous climbers in the animal kingdom are the monkeys. New World monkeys, that is, those that live in the Americas, have **prehensile tails**, with which they can grip the branches. The tamandua anteater and the North American tree porcupine use their tails in the same way, as do many of the possums in the northern Australian rain forests.

Old World monkeys, from Africa and Asia, do not have prehensile tails. However, they use their tails to steer when they are jumping from tree to tree. The colobus monkey, which lives in Africa, uses its beautiful plumed tail for this purpose. Many other tree-living animals, such as squirrels, have bushy tails to help them to jump.

Blond-crested woodpecker

Silky anteater

24

Monkeys and their relatives, such as lemurs, bushbabies and tarsiers, use their specially shaped hands and feet to grasp branches as they move around. The shape and position of their fingers vary, but each one is adapted for a particular purpose.

It seems strange to think of birds climbing, especially when they can fly perfectly well, but woodpeckers and tree-creepers need to be able to run up and down the trunks of trees to find food. They have sharp-clawed feet for gripping the bark, and short stiff tails, which support them while they are pecking at the bark in search of grubs. Parrots, too, climb among the branches as they feed, using their beaks and their feet for holding on.

Tree frogs have suckers on their toes, so that they can grip the slippery, shiny leaves of many rain forest trees. The disk-winged bat of Costa Rica also has suckers, on the corners of its wings. It uses these for holding onto a rolled-up leaf in which it roosts during the day.

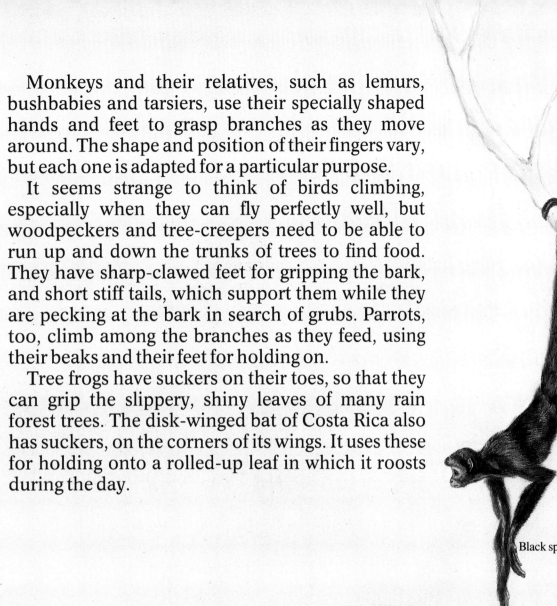

Black spider monkey

Tree frog
(Lutz's phyllomedusa)

25

Some adaptations for breeding

All animals are adapted in some way to ensure that they are successful in producing healthy young. One important adaptation to bad weather conditions is called delayed development.

Mammals that live in places where the winters are very cold, such as seals, sea otters, badgers and some deer, often mate in summer. This means that normally the young would be born in winter. However, their development inside their mother is delayed, so that they are not born until springtime.

Perhaps the most successful breeding adaptation is that of the kangaroos in Australia, where long **droughts** are very common. Kangaroos and their relatives, the wallabies, usually have three growing babies at one time. One is hopping around on the ground, a younger one is growing up inside the mother's pouch, and yet another is waiting as an **embryo** in her **uterus**. It will begin developing as soon as the baby kangaroo has left her pouch.

Kangaroos have successfully adapted their breeding patterns to suit the Australian climate.

Most birds with webbed feet cannot perch in branches. Red-footed boobies of the Galapagos Islands have become adapted to perch in shrubs, so that they can nest there. Their young are safer in the branches than on the ground, where most other seabirds make their nests.

If there is a drought, and food is hard to find for a long time, the mother abandons her two larger babies. The embryo inside her will not develop any further until the rains have returned. The mother mates as soon as this new baby is born, so that she has another embryo waiting inside her, ready for her pouch to be empty again. This method of breeding might seem cruel to humans, but it means that as soon as the drought is over, the kangaroo **population** will recover very quickly.

Cuckoos lay their eggs in other birds' nests and leave them there to be reared by the mother bird that made the nest. Cuckoos' eggs are always laid in nests of much smaller birds, perhaps a sparrow's or a wren's. To breed successfully in this way, the mother cuckoo must have two special adaptations. She must be able to lay her egg very quickly, while the nest's owner is away for a short while. She must also lay an egg that looks like those eggs already in the nest.

Adjusting to people and cities

Many animals have become adapted to living with people, in towns and cities as well as in the countryside. Some of them are found wherever people live: the house sparrow, the house mouse, the house spider and the housefly are found wherever there are humans, as their names suggest.

Any animal that can become used to people can enjoy a comfortable life, sheltering in their homes or eating scraps of food. People are often kind to animals such as birds and squirrels, putting out food for them in the garden.

Possums in Australia, like raccoons in the United States and Canada, have become so tame that they can sometimes be a nuisance around the house. In Europe, foxes come at night to raid trash cans, even in the big cities. In the town of Churchill, Manitoba, in Canada, polar bears come in during the winter, having learned that food is easy to find in trash cans and garbage dumps.

Right *For centuries birds of prey, like this falcon, have been trained by people to perform hunting tasks. However, they never become fully tame.*

Below *A family of adventurous polar bears raiding a garbage dump for food near Churchill, Manitoba, in Canada.*

Not all animals treat humans as a source of food. Kestrels and house martins use buildings as nesting places, as if they were cliff faces. In the town of Tromso, in northern Norway, small gulls called kittiwakes nest on the front of buildings in the main street, ignoring the traffic and the people below. Kittiwakes usually nest on cliffs near the sea.

Bats generally live in caves or hollow trees, but they are equally at home in the roof of a house or in a church tower. They might share their living space with barn owls in the country or starlings in a city.

One of the greatest behavioral adaptations was made by wild horses, cattle and dogs when they began to work for humans. Their wild relatives, however, are still afraid of people. All kinds of animals can be trained as pets, from snakes to wildcats and birds of prey. They have adapted their fierce natural behavior and have slowly learned to trust the humans who look after them.

Below *Possums live in the rain forest of Queensland, Australia. Some of them have become used to humans and will venture close to people's homes.*

Glossary

Altitude   Height above sea level.

Avalanche   A mass of snow that falls down a mountainside.

Carnivorous   Flesh-eating.

Competition   The struggle between plants or animals for space, light or food.

Concentration   The strength of a liquid.

Cramps   A painful temporary condition when the muscles contract uncontrollably.

Digest   To break down food that has been eaten, so that its nourishment can be absorbed into the body.

Dilute   Weak, containing much water.

Drought   A long period without rainfall.

Embryo   A young animal that is growing inside its mother's body.

Environment   An animal's surroundings including the soil, air, water, plants and other animals.

Evolution   The slow process by which animals change, over many generations, to suit their environment.

Evolved   Developed or changed to suit a particular purpose.

Gills   Organs that enable an animal to breathe under water.

Herbivores   Animals that eat only plants.

Insulation   A way of preventing the outside temperature from affecting an animal's own body temperature.

Larvae (singular larva)   The young form of insects after they hatch from the egg.

Mammals   Warm-blooded animals with hairy skins that feed their young on milk.

Migrate   To travel from one area to another as the seasons change.

Nocturnal   Active during the night.

Population   The numbers of a particular species.

Predators   Animals that live by eating other animals, which are their prey.

Prehensile tail   A flexible tail that is adapted for grasping branches.

Prey   An animal that is killed by another animal for food.

Rain forest   A dense forest of tall, broadleaved trees found in tropical regions.

Species   A group of animals or plants that is different from all other groups. The members of one species only breed with each other.

Streamlined   Having a simple, smooth shape that moves easily through the air or water.

Sweat glands   The organs of an animal that produce sweat.

Uterus   The part of a female mammal in which her baby develops before it is born. It is sometimes called a womb.

Picture acknowledgments

The publishers would like to thank the following for allowing their photographs to be reproduced in this book: Bruce Coleman Limited 4 (Allan Power), 7 (Kunio Takana/Orion Press), 18 (G Pizzey/WWF), 19 (Konrad Wothe); Oxford Scientific Films/Animals Animals 17, 28 (Richard Kolar); Survival Anglia Limited 23 (Jeff Foott), 27 (Dr. F. Koster). The diagram on page 16 (bottom right) is by Malcolm Walker.

Further information

To find out more about how animals are adapted to different environments, you might like to read the books suggested below:

Animal Camouflage by Malcolm Penny. The Bookwright Press, 1988.

Animal Disguises by Gwen Vevers. Merrimack Publishing Corp., distributed by Associated Booksellers, 1982.

Animal Evolution by Malcolm Penny. The Bookwright Press, 1987.

Animal Movement by Malcolm Penny. The Bookwright Press, 1987.

Animals in Winter by Ronald M. Fisher. The National Geographic Society, 1982.

Animals in your Neighborhood by Seymour Simon. Walker and Co., 1976.

Hunters and the Hunted: Surviving in the Animals World by Dorothy H. Patent. Holiday House, 1981.

Keeping Warm, Keeping Cool by Joan E. Rahn. Athaneum, 1983.

Night Animals by Wildlife Education Ltd. Published and distributed by them, 1984.

Secrets of Animal Survival by Donald J. Crump, Editor. The National Geographic Society, 1983.

There are many interesting wildlife films on television that show how animals have become adapted to their environment. Two excellent programs are *Life on Earth* and *The Living Planet*, which are also available as videos.

You can learn more about wild animals, and help to protect them, by joining one of the organizations listed below:

**Audubon Naturalist Society
of the Central Atlantic States**
8940 Jones Mill Road
Chevy Chase, Maryland 20815

The Conservation Foundation
1717 Massachusetts Avenue, N.W.
Washington, D.C. 20036

Greenpeace
1611 Connecticut Avenue, N.W.
Washington, D.C. 20009

The Humane Society of the USA
2100 L Street, N.W.
Washington, D.C. 20037

**The International Fund for
Animal Welfare**
P.O. Box 193
Yarmouth Port, Massachusetts 02675

National Wildlife Foundation
1412 16th Street, N.W.
Washington, D.C. 20036

The World Wildlife Fund
1255 23rd Street, N.W.
Washington, D.C. 20037

Index